Wh Words Go?

Ron Benson
Lynn Bryan
Kim Newlove
Liz Stenson
Iris Zammit

CONSULTANTS

Florence Brown
Estella Clayton
Susan Elliott-Johns
Charolette Player
Shari Schwartz
Lynn Swanson
Helen Tomassini
Debbie Toope

Prentice Hall Ginn

Contents

Alphabet Fun

by Kim Newlove

Illustrated by Barbara Reid

A and B and C and D
Are playing games down
by the sea.

E, F, and G, H, I
Are flying kites up in the sky.

4

J, K, L, and M, N, O
Are making people out of snow.

P, Q, R, S, T, and U
Are cooking up a vegetable stew.

V and W, X, Y, Z

Climb up the stairs and go to bed.

Where Do My Words Go?

by Donna Swan

Illustrated by Doris Barrette

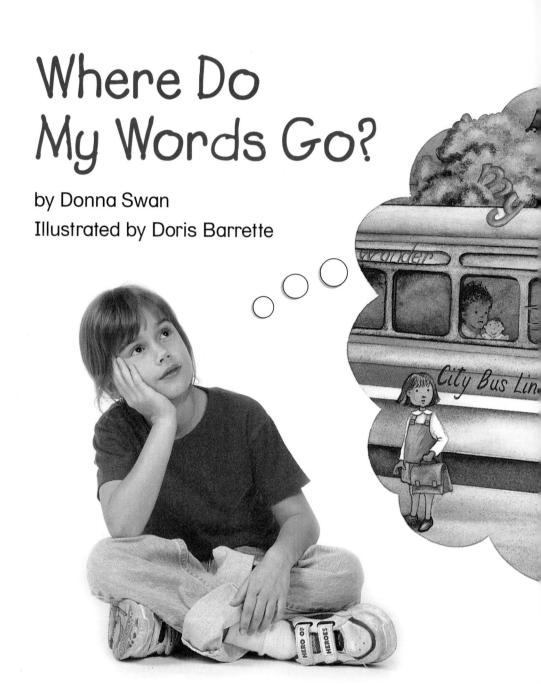

I wonder where my words go
when I talk.

Do they jump on a bus
and ride around town?

Do they bump into a tall tree
and get stuck in the branches?

Do they float up into the sky
and sit on the clouds?

I think I'll put my words
in a book so I can
keep them for ever and ever.

A Big Surprise

by Matthew Harris
Photographed by Chris Acton

Something exciting
happened today!

I sent my mom a note that said,
"When you come home I'll have
a big surprise for you!"

I sent my dad a note that said, "When you come home I'll have a big surprise for you!"

I called my aunt and told her,
"When you come home I'll have
a big surprise for you!"

When they came home,
they all asked, "What's the
big surprise?"

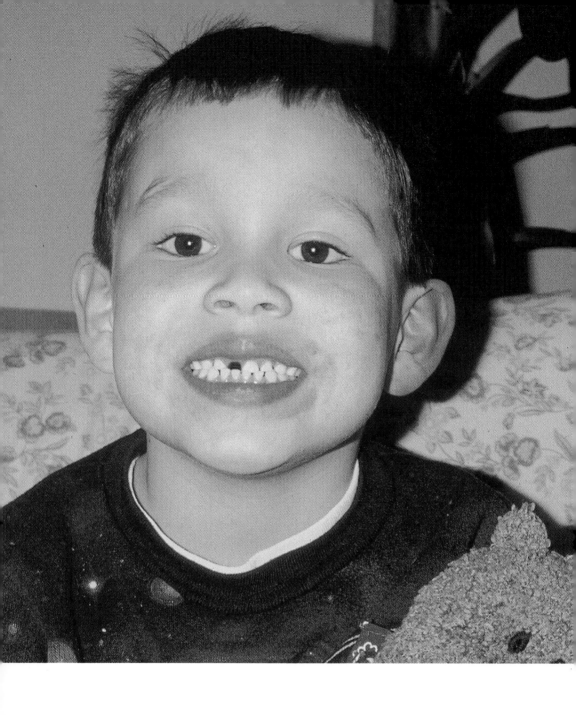

"My tooth came out today!"
I said.

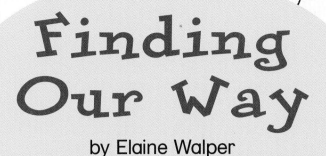

Finding Our Way

by Elaine Walper
Illustrated by Daniel Sylvestre

Words help us find our way
in school.
I can find the books.

Words help us find our way in the store.
I can find the milk.

Words help us find our way
in the food court.
I can find the pizza.

Words help us find our way around town.
I can find the street.

22

Words help us find our way
around the park.
I can find the lake.

Words help us find
a lot of things.
I can even find my friend!

24